Ednah Dow Littlehale Cheney, Harriet Winslow Sewall

Poems

Ednah Dow Littlehale Cheney, Harriet Winslow Sewall

Poems

ISBN/EAN: 9783744704946

Printed in Europe, USA, Canada, Australia, Japan

Cover: Foto ©Thomas Meinert / pixelio.de

More available books at **www.hansebooks.com**

POEMS

BY

HARRIET WINSLOW SEWALL

WITH A MEMOIR BY

EDNAH D. CHENEY

CAMBRIDGE
Printed at the Riverside Press
1889

CONTENTS.

———◆———

FANCY.

HARRIET WINSLOW SEWALL.

When the roses of summer droop before the heats of August or the coming frosts of autumn, we gather the fair and perfumed petals and preserve them in a rare and costly vase, that the fragrance may remain with us through the dark, cold days of winter. So, when a being as fair, pure, and beautiful as the summer roses she loved so dearly passes from our earthly sight, we long to gather up the leaves that have fallen and preserve her memory ever with us.

How little of all the varied melody of her life is phonographed on these few papers which are left to us! And yet, when these characters from her hand find a chord so delicately tuned that it can vibrate in unison, the voice of the song will again be heard, and young hearts will thrill to the music of her life, while those who have listened to these poems from her own lips will hear again that trembling cadence which gave expression to every shade of thought.

We treasure all that remains to us of this rare and exquisite, this "unique" product of Nature. Harriet Winslow Sewall seems to have won from long lines of life, purity, fineness, grace, and tenderness, blended with transparent truth and fidelity to right and duty. We can hardly think of her alone, but see at her side the venerable figure of her husband, with whom she lived in ever-deepening love and trust for more than thirty years. Strength and beauty, courage and tenderness, were so blended in them that respect and love were their equal and immediate tribute.

We seek to know the origin of a being so gifted and so harmonious. Harriet Winslow was born in Portland, June 30, 1819. She was the youngest daughter of Nathan and Com-

fort Hussey Winslow, who were both of Quaker
origin. Thankful Hussey, the grandmother, was
a noted Quaker preacher. Harriet was brought
up in the Society of Friends, in that atmosphere
of serene piety and pure morality which distin-
guishes households of that persuasion. She attended school in Portland, and also the Friends'
boarding-school in Providence. But while something of the sweet influences of Quakerism
always lingered about her, in the quiet uncon-
sciousness of her manners and the direct sim-
plicity of her thought, she was by no means fet-
tered by the severe restrictions of her sect, but
her earliest conscious life flowed out into beauty
and song as naturally as that of the flowers and
the birds. The beautiful world about her was
a never-failing source of delight, and harmony
in her dress and all the appointments of her
life a necessity to her. She never lost her delight in the " poetry of motion," and dancing
was a relief when she was lonely or sad. Some
pleasant verses by Miss Whittier show how her

friends felt about the defection of the sisters
from the Friends' society : —

A LAMENT FOR THE GRAND-DAUGHTERS OF THANKFUL
HUSSEY.

Where now is our Louisa ?[1]
Where now is our Louisa ?
Where now is our Louisa ?
　　　Wandered from the Quaker rest.

She went out by habeas corpus,
She went out by habeas corpus,
She went out by habeas corpus,
　　　From the Quaker fold and rest.

Where now is Lucy Ellen ?
Where now is Lucy Ellen ?
Where now is Lucy Ellen ?
　　　Stolen from the Quaker rest.

She went out by the guile o' Foxes,[2]
She went out by the guile o' Foxes,
She went out by the guile o' Foxes,
　　　Stolen from the Quaker rest.

[1] Married to a lawyer, Samuel E. Sewall, Esq.
[2] Married to Mr. (afterwards Judge) Edward Fox.

Where now is sister Hatty ?[1]
Where now is sister Hatty ?
Where now is sister Hatty ?
   Wandering from the Quaker rest.

She 'll go out from Falmouth Quarter,
She 'll go out from Falmouth Quarter,
She 'll go out from Falmouth Quarter,
   Dancing from the Quaker rest.

Where now are the three sisters ?
Where now are the three sisters ?
Where now are the three sisters ?
   Wanderers from the Quaker rest.

By and by they 'll all be turning,
By and by they 'll all be turning,
By and by they 'll all be turning,
   Wearied, to the Quaker rest.

Fifth day eve'g, 31st.

Her girlhood in her father's home was rich and happy. She entered into the intellectual life of the " Transcendental " period, and writes of the poems that were dear to her. She was attracted by the weird influences of animal mag-

---

[1] Afterwards Harriet Winslow Sewall.

netism, and is disposed rather to accept than to criticise and reject. She writes in 1842 : " But to return to magnetism. It is a subject in which I am exceedingly interested. How can any one laugh at it? It opens a door to higher regions. I have been reading Townsend's book. The Americans must be deficient in some essential faculty that they can be so insensible on such an interesting subject. Some ridicule it, others fear it. They regard it as coming from the Devil, and contrary to all the laws of Nature. As if all the laws of Nature had ever been discovered! Why, there are more things in heaven and earth than common philosophy ever dreams of. Have we become so all-wise that we should be no longer seekers? If past ages had done the same, where would be our present improvements? You think of Transcendentalism as of some horrid bugbear, which is in truth one of your own creating. You speak of their God and the Christians' as two different things. Oh, believe me, we are all

seeking after the one true God. I trust we
shall all find Him sooner or later, though we
may take different paths. I am grateful, dear
Harriet, for your kind admonition. I know I am
erring and weak, but do not attribute my failings to Transcendentalism. Inasmuch as I am
not holy, I am not transcendental. Yet oh, how
I love holiness, how I love purity! and loving
and aspiring as I do, may I not hope to be something better? If I cannot go to heaven, I will
go no other way ; that I am resolved."

But she does not lose herself in speculation.
The stern demands upon conscience from the
anti - slavery movement had a bracing effect,
which saved many a young soul from becoming
lost in fancy and sentimentalism.

Her early interest in the woman movement
is shown by a burlesque letter written to Mr.
Sewall in 1838 in the name of her baby niece.
Her sister, the wife of Mr. Sewall, had been
obliged to attend some case in court as a witness,
and the baby thus complains : —

MY DEAR PAPA, — I have been strongly impressed for the last week with the fallacy of Miss Martineau's reasoning, and all the new-fangled notions about woman's rights and woman's sphere; and finding it impossible to induce any one here to listen to good common sense, I turn to you, dear papa, as a last resource. Things are going on here which meet my decided disapprobation. Here is mamma day after day going to court, and coming home with her head full of pleas, and charges, and evidence, and juries, etc., etc., so that she can talk about nothing else. It is just so with all the other women. They are leaving their appropriate sphere and meddling with affairs they do not understand, and I assure you, dear papa, this state of things is a great shock to my intuitive ideas of female propriety. And to think my dear mamma should be so misled !

When she goes out, I cling to her and say, " Baby too, baby too," but all in vain. She tells me she is going to court and gives me over to Aunt Hatty, who I confess does not disgrace her sex so shamelessly as the rest. I write to warn you, my dear papa, for I strongly suspect that when mamma goes home she intends to place you in the nursery to take care of me, and attend to the other female duties, and will take all your business into her own hands.

She will attribute this usurpation, I dare say, to a regard for your health, for she complains daily of the bad air at the court-house, and wonders how you have been able to endure it. I have no doubt she compassionates you, but do not be deceived, for I have an innate horror of seeing a woman rule over her husband. How mortified I should be, on my return to Boston, when any one should inquire for mamma! I should have to say, "Mamma is gone to *office ;*" and when they asked for papa I should have to reply, "He is mending mamma's clothes." Oh the degeneracy of womankind! But I will not dwell longer on this painful subject.

I begin to have a better opinion of phrenology and of Mr. Combe. His ideas upon education are very fine, and evince a great deal of observation; particularly the management of children, if I have heard mamma state them rightly. He thinks the combativeness and destructiveness of children should never be excited by contradiction or by crosses of any kind, and I agree with him exactly. I think he must have been a child himself once. For myself, I always feel a propensity to scream and kick when my wishes are not attended to, as the only way of enforcing obedience; and I am sure it would be much better policy to attend to me at first, and save me all the expense of tears and muscular effort.

I long to see you very much, my dear papa, and to kiss you. I shall have many wonderful things to tell you when I return, and many pretty things to show. One thing which fills me with astonishment is that, notwithstanding my extensive knowledge and acquirements, there is not a day passes but I learn something new. I am ready to exclaim, " What cannot woman's intellect grasp ! "

I send a great deal of love to grandpa and to Aunt Hannah. Mamma has just come from court, and I must bid you by-by.

Lucy Ellen Sewall.

This letter recalls an interesting feature of the great Presidential struggle of 1840 : —

Portland [*August* or *September*], 1840.

Dear Louisa. — We have had a great Whig convention here, and all the Whig houses were full of the delegates, so we came in for a small share. From early in the morning the town was as busy as a bee-hive, with the rattling of all sorts of vehicles, and the continual ingress of countrymen and strangers. The Thorn came from Brunswick with *four hundred* passengers on board. I wonder where they got the wherewithal to feed them. We were honored with seven to dine with us, four of them modest young men, whom perhaps *you* might have induced to talk, but I could not. They were as dumb as puppets, and came and went without making a very deep im-pression on anybody. How I wished you were here to bring out their inner man ! The ladies here take an unusual interest in politics, and run to hear the great speakers, and talk very learnedly about mat-ters that I cannot understand. I have not caught the mania. I had just curiosity enough to take a peep at Erastus Brooks, who was speechifying on the State House steps to the assembled multitude ; but I was not much electrified, for his voice did not reach me, and as I could only see his passionate gestures, which were not quite so expressive as the " Invisible Harlequin's," I was rather moved to laughter.

While Miss Winslow delighted in every form
of beauty, the art in which she found expression
most easily was poetry. How early she began
to voice her feelings in numbers we do not
know, but some of her verses which remain were
certainly written before 1836, when she was
seventeen years old, and the greater number of
them within the next twenty-three years before
1859. Her most celebrated poem, beginning,

" Why thus longing, thus forever sighing ? "

which so happily expressed the feeling of the
young, ardent spirits of her time, was written
during her girlhood and published in 1840. It
met with immediate response, and has been in-
cluded in all collections of the best American
poetry. It is a gem whose thought has crystal-
lized into perfect beauty. She thus speaks of
the publication : —

1840.

. . . I was surprised to see my verses so soon.
I am glad you sent them, if it were only for the pleasure they gave to mother when she read them in print

with the accompanying eulogy. I did not follow your advice to republish them, for I think some of the corrections are for the better, and the mistakes are so palpable that any intelligent reader would take them for such. In the verse commencing, "If no dear eyes," the measure was not perfect before, and I suppose it jarred on his poetical ear, but I think he has sacrificed the sense to the measure. I 'm obstinately opposed to those "fragrant fields," inasmuch as the sense of smelling is inferior to that of seeing. On the whole, I made quite a figure in the " World," did n't I ?

In the summer of 1848 Miss Winslow married a young German who had been in the office of Mr. Sewall. Charles List had come to this country while still a boy, and worked very hard to acquire an education and a profession. He had fine intellectual powers and large literary attainments, and a fair promise of success in life. But the bright hopes of the young couple were soon overcast, for hardly had they returned from the wedding journey when symptoms of a fearful disease, which left no hope of relief or cure, appeared in the young husband.

As long as possible Mr. List toiled on, being engaged on the " Commonwealth " newspaper; but he was at last obliged to relinquish it, and had no resource for support. Mrs. List made every effort by teaching music to sustain herself and husband, but, untrained to a profession, she found it impossible. Her father's means were not large, but he assisted her through this trying period. The poor sufferer was either in a hospital or in a quiet country place. His wife watched over him devotedly, reading to him and contributing to his comfort in every possible way.

This playful letter to her niece shows how she found pleasure and amusement even in the most unpromising surroundings : —

CONGIN, *Monday* [about 1853].

DEAR LUCY, — I was pleased to read such a pleasant account of your Christmas tree, but you ought to have mentioned all the presents that you and Lulu had. I should like to have been there to see the children's delight. I found a great deal of pleasure in making the children here some little presents, for they so seldom have any it is a great treat to them. And they have been so obliging, and so ready to do us any little service, that I was glad for an occasion to give them pleasure. I am sorry to say they sometimes quarrel among themselves, and the older boys tyrannize too much over the younger ones. It is unaccountable to me that the consciousness of power does not bring a sentiment of forbearance towards the weak. It is so mean to take advantage of one's strength.

We had some fine sport on the ice yesterday. The last rain joined to the melting snow made a beautiful pond on the interval, which froze over and gave us the nicest place to slide you can imagine. It was smooth as glass. After sliding on my feet awhile, Augustus brought along an old waiter, worn out in service, which he had been trying to go down hill upon, and said he would give me a ride. I seated myself on the waiter, and he gave me one end of his scarf to hold and pulled with the other. He is such a little fellow I did not think he could pull me, but

after we were started, he had to run fast to keep the
waiter from running over him. So he rode me all
round the pond. I should have mentioned that Augustus had on rubbers, which enabled him to run without slipping, though the rest of us could not. It was
the nicest sleigh-ride I ever had. I fancied I went
like a Laplander with a little reindeer. I got Mrs.
Lewis to come out and take a ride, too. Mr. List was
there, but only looked on. We thought it would be
fine to go out by moonlight. When the moon rises
over the interval it makes a beautiful scene. But it
grew cloudy at night, and now our crystal pond is
covered with a light snow. I wish I knew how to
skate. If I thought I could learn I would try.

Since I wrote you, I went to a village dance at
Sacarappa. We danced schottisches, and quadrilles,
and contra dances, and Spanish, and waltzes; in short,
all that you find in the big cities, and a little more.
But we had more room, and there was more sociability.
I danced every dance but the first, and felt very soon
acquainted. The Lewises' doctor was there, whom
I had become some acquainted with from his visits to
the family. He is a very pleasant man, and I danced
with him several times. Mrs. Lewis had told him

that I did not eat meat, and he said I might enjoy
tolerable health, but I could not be so strong as those
that used meat, to which I replied by boasting that I
was as strong as he. It was the next night I met him
at the dance. When I am dancing those dances that
have no particular limit to them, like the schottische,
with gentlemen, I always propose to stop after a little
while, for fear I may tire them out; if a lady, I know
she will say if she is tired, but a gentleman don't like
to confess it first. So when I danced the schottische
with the doctor, after going round the hall once, I
proposed to stop. He concluded I was tired, and
said he was a little so. I replied playfully that I was
not tired at all, that I never knew what fatigue was
in dancing, but I knew it was not so with meat-eaters,
and I always stopped out of pity to them. He re-
membered his advice the day before, and seemed to
enjoy the retort. A little while after, he had been
waltzing with a lady and complained of being dizzy,
and asked me if it was because he ate meat, and said
he should certainly prepare himself for the next dance
by a vegetable dinner. I waltzed with a young lady
who was the easiest person I ever found to waltz
with. The music was beautiful, and I enjoyed it very

much. One part of the tune seemed to lift us off our feet.

I enjoyed your account of the picnic at Halifax, and sympathized with you very keenly when your throat was burning with the peppery hotch-potch. Did you get any salt-fish while you were gone? Do you have your piano in town? Give my love to Mary and Fanny.   HATTY.

This paragraph was written at a later period but refers to the time when, for a few months, she lived with Mr. List in an almost unfurnished house in Pennsylvania : —

[*October* or *November*, 1862.]

DEAR HATTY, — Poverty certainly has its delights. I remember, in Pennsylvania, with what gusto I used to view my dressing-table, which was a barrel turned upside down. Chairs were a great superfluity. I did not even have a bed, and slept so well I have had an enmity to beds ever since. Whether it was the novelty of the thing that made it charming, I cannot say, but

" When summer comes, with bloom and song,
When dawns are rosy and days are long,"

I always feel that I should like to burn the house up and live in the woods.

Mrs. Sewall's mother, to whom she was most tenderly attached, died in 1843, and soon after her only brother. In 1850 her sister Louisa (Mrs. Sewall) died very suddenly. Mr. List died in April, 1856. Her last sister, Ellen, a very lovely person, died soon after Mr. List. These bereavements made this the one unhappy portion of her life. The sensitiveness of her nervous constitution caused her to suffer so keenly from bereavement that her friends were filled with anxiety for her health ; but she rallied finally to fresh influences, and found new happiness in life after every loss. In 1856 she wonders " if heaven can be more beautiful than earth."

Mrs. Sewall was very fond of children, and always liked to have them about her. This letter shows the kind of family life she longed for : —

Sunday morning [1855.]

My DEAR COUSIN, — I delight in a large family. I wish I could gather all my relations together under

one great roof ; then what a formidable front we could
oppose to all evils! Care and sickness should not
enter, and Death, how could he carry any one off when
so many hands would be ready to hold the beloved
one back! One of my favorite castles in the air, for
many years, has been the building of a great castle
on the earth, in which money has been of no account,
I have had so much, and in which I have provided
the most beautiful accommodations for all my friends.
I assure thee, dear cousin, there is the most beautiful
room for thee there, and in a little alcove the choicest
collection of books. If you were in want of pupils,
I would be one. I am sadly ignorant of many things,
and among others would like to study astronomy of
thee. I forbear giving thee a full description of this
fair abode, lest it should make thee entirely dissatisfied
with thy present, but thee must hold thyself in readi-
ness, when my air castle gets a solid foundation, to
come and live in it.

Such fair fruits shall adorn my table as have never
been seen since the days of Eden, and the meat offer-
ings (for I would not force my friends into vegetarian-
ism) shall be so hidden by roses as not to mar the
banquet by their unsightliness. And oh, better than

wine will be the mirth and joy that goes round the circle. But, alas! in our "isolated households" we can have but a poor idea of social enjoyment.

But there is one poor creature for whom there is no room even in her Paradise. She goes on to say : —

I have generally slept pretty well, and when I have been kept awake it has been by mosquitoes. If Dr. S. has any medicine that will keep them off, do beg him to send it directly, or something that will put them to sleep. Their song is worse than the howling of wolves. I have been very much amused with the book the doctor lent me, and Mr. Sewall is quite taken with it. I have great sympathy with all visionary people, and am always half inclined to believe the wildest things that are strongly insisted upon ; for when we think of this miracle of life, what should seem impossible to us ? Have we not realized what past generations deemed impossible and ridiculous ? But I have more faith in removing all cause of sorrow from the world than in taking *ignatia* to cure it.

One of Mrs. Sewall's strongest traits was her

love of nature. She drank in the beauty of the world at every breath. She writes thus to her niece : —

GERMANTOWN, PA., *Sunday morning, June 1st.*

DEAR LUCY, — I think this is the most enticing season out-of-doors, when everything is growing and rejoicing, and the sun warms without melting you. Here it is perfectly lovely. I wonder if heaven can be more beautiful than these green spots of earth, where trees, and flowers, and birds, and springing grass, and overarching sky, mingling in an endless variety of ways, afford us ever new delight. They talk of the jasper walls of heaven, as if any walls could be so beautiful as these outlets into eternal space, draperied with luxuriant foliage swaying in the breeze! For curtains give me the drooping willows. Do you remember those graceful groups of willows by Church Lane and Mrs. Pugh's beautiful grounds? How pleasant they make the walk to the depot! I wish there was something of the kind at Melrose. The moment I get out of the cars here, I am refreshed and rested by the sight of the shade and foliage.

In 1857 she was married to Mr. Sewall, with whom she lived in the sweetest communion and confidence for more than thirty years.

In 1861 Mrs. Sewall's father died, leaving her a moderate fortune. She enjoyed the freedom it gave her to carry out her own plans, although her generous husband was always ready to fulfill her wishes. In 1859 we have this characteristic passage on tragedy : —

MELROSE, *Sunday afternoon* [1859].

MY DEAR COUSIN, — Last evening we read aloud the third part of " White Lies." I think it has been the most entertaining work Reade has written so far, and I should extol it highly if we had not just come to some tragedy, which I detest. As if we had not enough of it in real life, but must have even our amusements stuffed with it! If I were senator, I would introduce a law for the abolishment and annihilation of all tragedies, and make it a criminal offense to write one.

She certainly did not shrink from effort or suffering when it came in the path of duty, but her sensitive soul did not like to dwell upon it, and she would have led mankind upward by light and joy, rather than by the stern discipline of sorrow.

Mr. and Mrs. Sewall spent their summers at their beautiful country home at Melrose, sharing in all the interests of the town, and in winter they had apartments in Park Street, Boston, near Mr. Sewall's office and the rooms of the New England Women's Club, where with simple, elegant hospitality they received their old anti-slavery friends and others, who helped to make their "life the feast it was." Visits to friends in Portland, Philadelphia, and other places broke the routine of their lives. Work and play were alike refreshing to them.

Mrs. Sewall occasionally wrote poems through these years, but she never made literature a steady pursuit. She had no personal ambition, no aspiration for fame, and she expresses her wonder that Miss Landor could passionately long for an earthly immortality. A few of her

poems were printed in the " Commonwealth"
when Mr. List edited it, but she never took any
pains to collect and publish them, and wrote only
from the impulse of her own feeling or the re-
quest of friends.

In 1883 she collected and arranged the letters of her friend, Lydia Maria Child, in a most
satisfactory manner, but would not suffer her
name to appear on the title-page.

She engaged in philanthropic work, and
showed an amount of practical ability which
was a surprise to those who had thought of her
only as a poetic dreamer.

Mr. Sewall's position in regard to slavery, as
well as her own feelings, must have made the
period preceding and during the War of Rebel-
lion one of the greatest excitement and interest.
This account of the Festival of Emancipation
shows what relief that great event brought to
them : —

MELROSE, *January* 11, 1863.

I cannot write the date of this memorable year, dear Hatty, without congratulating you and myself and the whole nation upon the great event with which it commences. What if not a single slave is freed by it, we still have the immense satisfaction of washing our hands as a country clean of the curse, of feeling that we really have a country worth struggling for. On New Year's Day there was a grand concert given at Music Hall in honor of the great event, and the flower of the State was assembled. We had a seat in the first balcony, not far from the stage, so that we had a fine view both of the audience and the performers. The entertainment was opened by a poem from Emerson, — short but very fine. The music was very choice, vocal and instrumental, some of Beethoven's finest pieces, to which his beautiful bronze statue with head inclined seemed attentively listening. In one of the pauses it was announced that the proclamation was passing over the wires, which was received with immense cheering. The gentlemen rose and swung their hats, the ladies waved their handkerchiefs. It was thrilling to see how the hearts of that great assembly seemed to beat as

one. Then three cheers were proposed for Abraham
Lincoln, and three more for William Lloyd Garri-
son, both of which received an enthusiastic response.
This was in the afternoon. In the evening Mr.
Sewall and I were invited to a select party at Mr.
Stearns's, in Medford, where we met Garrison, Phillips, Emerson, Alcott, Mrs. Julia Ward Howe, Mrs.
Severance, Samuel Longfellow, Sanborn, Brackett the
sculptor, and a few others. Emerson read his poem
again, for the benefit of some who were too far off,
in the afternoon, to hear well. The marble bust of
John Brown, which has been at the Athenæum for a
long time, had just been brought home, — you know
Stearns employed Brackett to take it. Mr. Phillips
made a little speech in honor of its inauguration,
and Sanborn read a poem. I have seldom enjoyed
any party so much.

Both Mr. and Mrs. Sewall were among the
first members of the New England Women's
Club, founded in 1868, and in a few years she
became its treasurer. She managed its finances
with great skill, and by her tact and economy
put them on a firm footing. She also served on

the business committee. A letter to an absent member of the club gives a hint of her work. Mr. Sewall joked her on her very unselfish methods of business, but she maintained that her plans were good for herself, as well as for the club. She wrote several occasional poems, full of fun and satire, and often took part in discussions, always adding wit and wisdom to the conversation.

"Mr. Sewall always has a sly laugh when they praise my financial abilities, because, he says, 'I gave the club the interest from investments, and made no account of the stock's falling afterwards;' but the fact is, both I and the club are richer for the investments."

In March, 1873, Mrs. Sewall was elected on the school committee for the town of Melrose for the term of one year, and in March, 1874, she was reëlected for three years, and served until December, 1874, when she resigned.

She entered as heartily into the varied work of the Educational and Industrial Union, espe-

cially the legal department for the protection
of women in contracts for labor. Of her private
charities we will not speak. They are known,
as she wished them to be, only to the recipients.

A few extracts from her correspondence will
give some idea of the course of her life and
thoughts: —

BOSTON, *June* 11, 1874.

DEAR HATTY, — I have not had any chance to
commence another sheet of journal to you, there
have been so many letters to answer, but almost every
day I have had talks with you in spirit. How I wish
they could be photographed, it would be such a
saving of eyesight and time! You would not say
then that my letters were short. . . .

It was April in temperature and the walking perfectly dry, for many previous days of rain and thaw
had carried off all the snow, and had washed away
all sins from the earth, I think, so lovely everything
and everybody looked. I went out to see the Welds
in the afternoon. They seemed well, though Mrs.
Weld is not strong, and I had a delightful call. Mr.
Weld insisted upon returning to the depot with me,

and it was a memorable walk. In addition to the
lovely day, which made mere existence enjoyment,
Mr. Weld's inspiring words lifted me into spiritual
regions. Our talk turned upon Miss Grimké, and he
said with such fervor that he not merely believed, but
he knew, that her beautiful and noble life continued,
that I felt I could trust to his sight, though I myself was blind. May his life long be spared to elevate the lives of others! I went into the Swedenborg
circle yesterday, and found Mr. Alcott talking to the
ladies. He was quite eloquent, for women always inspire him, he says, and they seemed much interested
in his talk. He told them that men were much less
than they might be, because women demanded so little
of them. They were satisfied with too low a stand-
ard. I mentally repeated Patmore's lines : —

> "And favors that make Folly bold
> Put out the light in Virtue's face."

MELROSE, *June* 30, 1883.

MY DEAR HARRIET, —Your letter brought up
very pleasantly and vividly those old days, when I
looked upon every new abolitionist as a link between
men and angels, and the prominent ones as already

divine. What a thrill of wonder and rapture I should
have felt had I known that Mrs. Child and Mr. Weld
in some future year would dine with me regularly
once a week! I regarded the attention you paid
me at that time as great condescension, and did not
realize that we should one day seem of the same age.

MELROSE, *July* 4.

MY DEAR HARRIET, . . . May you find rest and
vigor and enjoy many birthdays, and each should be
happier than the last, because you will be nearer
heaven, and will have glimpses of it with your fine
spiritual sense! I cannot even conceive of happiness
that is not much like earth, and it will be very in-
complete if I do not have some tête-à-têtes with you,
but our gossip will be of a lofty kind.

October 30, 1884.

MY DEAR HARRIET,— You are like an oasis in
a desert to-day, for in the midst of a wearisome round
of packing I sit down and rest and refresh myself
by communion with you. I am always reminded, at
this season of moving, when tired with a hundred
things to look after, of the sick sultan whose doctor

told him he must find a happy man and wear his
shirt; and after long search the happy man was found,
but, alas! he had not a shirt to his back. Enviable
creature! And yet if one of my trunks should be lost
on the way to Boston, I should probably cry; un-
like *mein lieber Herr*, who, when his trunk was lost on
one of our journeys, summed up the pros and cons,
and made out, like " Hans in Luck," that on the whole
he was a great gainer. . . .

This is an exciting week, and Mr. Sewall thinks all
will come out right next Tuesday, but I have not the
happy faculty of believing what I want to, nor of
comforting myself with the maxim, " Whatever is, is
right." Part of the process of evolution is to make
mistakes and find them out, but oh, they are so dread-
ful sometimes!

Sunday, May 27, 1888.

DEAR LUCY, — Mr. Whittier has said that a visitor at Philadelphia has to *eat* his way through the city,
and I want to tell you how victoriously your father
has gone through the ten days of unwearying effort in
that line and come home safe and sound. Either
through innocence of what was offered, or a dislike of

saying No, he has met everything that came unflinch-
ingly, and you can imagine my panic to see him en-
counter deviled lobster (he will not even eat *plain*
at home), deviled crab, and nameless dishes of sus-
picious ingredients, and top off with ice-cream and
strawberries that this year are not ripe anywhere.
When invited out, I was not placed near enough to
him to give warning, and I suspect he sometimes res-
olutely avoided my eye. My anxiety was the only
drawback to my enjoyment, and now it is a great
satisfaction to think how strong he must be to do so
much with impunity.

Wednesday was a rather wearying day, for we had
delayed our calls on account of the weather, and they
must all be made at once. Emily ordered the carriage for our early return, as she knew we would be
tired, and we got back at 9.30, and I said to your
father, "I am going right to bed. Won't you come?
for I am so tired, and you must be." "Tired!" he
replied; "not at all, and I can't think of going to
bed at half past nine." I was pleased to hear him
say so, and I tell you all this because you will be glad,
too.

Mrs. Sewall was small and delicate in person, with a free, light, graceful carriage and action. She did not seem to walk, but rather to flit or glide along the streets, as if she did not belong to them. Her fair complexion, blue eyes, and loosely curling hair, often bound with a ribbon of blue, kept the appearance of girlhood to the verge of old age. She once acted "The fair maid with silver locks" when the silver was all her own. She was full of fresh, joyous life, and never lost the sparkle and gladness of youth. She danced like Perdita, as if she were a wave of the sea, and sang like a lark because it was morning. As late as 1885 she writes : —

151 Boylston St.

DEAR LUCY, — I find this a capital place to write my letters, — no interruptions (I am sorry to say), and the precious patent pen Mrs. Pitman gave me is very convenient. When I am tired of writing and reading, I sing and dance for exercise.

Mr. Sewall shared in all her interests and pleasures, and loved to watch her graceful motions in dance or frolic. He had great respect for her practical powers and said, " Hatty could do anything. She's a genius."

While the growing tremulousness of Mr. Sewall's manner and the increasing spiritual delicacy of his expression were evident, his step was yet so light and free, his mind so true, and his spirit so bright, that we scarcely thought of him as losing in health and vigor until he was suddenly stricken down by an acute attack of pneumonia. He struggled with his usual courage against disease, but could not rally from the attack, and died on December 20, 1888.

Mrs. Sewall bore this sudden and heavy blow with sweet patience, trying very soon to meet her friends and to resume her wonted occupations; but it was soon evident that the shock of bereavement was telling severely upon her nerves, and she was unable to sleep.

Acceding to the wish of her physician, she sought a little change in a visit to a dear cousin in the country. Here nature seemed to minister

to her with something of its old power of calm-
ing and refreshing, and her friends hoped for
restoration, but in a moment all earthly hopes
were destroyed. As she was walking near the
house, she crossed a railroad track, when an ex-
press train dashed by, and left her lifeless on the
ground.

Her friends tried to be consoled by the
thought that the passage from life was instan-
taneous, and that earth had little left for her to
desire. Her memory remains to them in unsul-
lied purity, a light, a joy, and a help.

These poems, which have been selected by the
daughters to give to her friends a lasting me-
morial of her exquisite life, did not receive her
revision, except as she wrote them out for a gift
for her husband; but in the selection the editors
have kept constantly in view what they believe
would have been Mrs. Sewall's wish in regard to
their publication. Many whole poems, and in a
few cases some stanzas of a poem, have been
omitted, from technical defects, but what is given

is almost without alteration.   Her friends will pardon an occasional roughness or fault of metre, for the sake of having her own words.

These poems need no critical analysis; they speak for themselves, from the heart to the heart.   They will be precious to those who feel in accord with the noble, loving writer, and carry her influence to those who had not the privilege of knowing her in life.

EDNAH D. CHENEY.

JAMAICA PLAIN, *November* 28, 1889.

POEMS TO S. E. S.

SONG.

When the golden and rose-tinted banners of
    morning
  Announce the approach of the bountiful
    day,
I think how its radiance thy room is adorn-
    ing,
  And I send thee a greeting on each golden
    ray.
  Good morning, Belovéd, good morning, good
    day,
      May they softly caress thee,
      And gladden and bless thee,
  And linger around thee, as I would alway.

And again when long shadows the night are
    foretelling,
  And eve is unveiling her mysteries afar,

The same dark blue dome overarches thy
    dwelling,
  And our glances can meet in the same sil-
    ver star.
  Good evening, Belovéd, good evening, good
    night,
      May the blue skies above thee,
      That lean to and love thee,
  Grow bluer as signal when thou art in
    sight.

TO MY DEAREST FRIEND.

(With a Manuscript Copy of her Verses.)

I KNOW what dear and loving eyes
    Will on these pages fall and linger,
With favoring glances fate denies
    To many a more successful singer.

So I collect my songs for thee
    Emboldened by this sweet assurance,
Foreseeing what their fate will be
    By thy love's lenient, long endurance.

For into tenderer hands than thine
    Could never frailty be committed,
Their worth will be o'erprized, like mine,
    Their failings will be only pitied.

And happier I with such applause,
    Than warrior on his homeward marches,

Returning from victorious wars,
  And rolling 'neath triumphal arches.

So dear, and far beyond my due
  Thy praises sweet, than laurels better,
If thou my gift approving view,
  The donor thou, and I the debtor.

TO S. E. S.

I PLEASE myself in lonely hours
  By fancying what sweet joy 't would be,
Oh dearest friend, could I requite thee
  For all that thou hast been to me.

Not only for sweet favors given,
  For care and counsel sweeter far,
For love that lifts the veil of heaven,
  And shows us what its glories are; —

Oh, not for these alone I thank thee;
  I bless thee from my inmost heart,
Not only for what thou hast given,
  But even more for what thou art.

My faith in goodness is made firmer,
  My hopes of what mankind may be

To loftier soarings are encouraged,
   Belovéd, when I think of thee.

And if my faith a moment fail me,
   When outward wrongs my credence claim,
And doubts and weaknesses assail me,
   They vanish if I breathe thy name.

And how could sorrow be surmounted,
   Belovéd, unless shared with thee,
By thy endearing love surrounded,
   And thy sustaining sympathy.

Oh, love may spring in sunny weather,
   In smiling bowers may bloom and grow,
But only those who weep together
   Its sweetest, holiest spell can know.

I LOVE THEE.

(Translated from the German for his Birthday.)

I THINK o'er and o'er all that language af-
    fords
For what I can send thee of winsomest
    words.
I search for the most honey sweet and select,
Now one, now another I choose and reject;
But when I would send them they suit me
    but ill,
For something far sweeter occurs to me still.

To my darling some beautiful gift I would
    send,
I seek, and select, and discard without end.
Now a flower it shall be and some verses to
    fit,
Now a ring to betoken truth inviolate;

But when I would send it again, I demur,
For something far fitter will surely occur.

I seek the world over for words to portray
How dear thou art to me, and dearer each
        day;
No sweet combination yet find I more fond
Than the fervent "I love thee," the truth
        unadorned.
Shall I seek for a tenderer, sweeter refrain?
Ah no! for I surely should seek it in vain.

DEPARTURE.

Long time I lingered at the window, watching
  Thy parting progress and the approaching
    storm;
The night came swiftly down as thou wert
  leaving,
  And folded round thy fast retreating form.

I wished I were the winds that followed after,
  And round thy footsteps fondly seemed to
    play;
Oh! I should chase all evil from thy path-
  way,
  And treat thee with more reverence than
    they.

I thought of many a form in which to follow,
  And hover round thee, over land and sea;
I yielded to these fancies that kept thronging,
  To still the longing that I felt for thee.

I opened many a book that thou hadst brought
    me,
  Rich with all nature's lore and melody;
I tried the favorite songs that time had
    taught me, —
  No book, no song, so sweet as thoughts of
    thee.

Though impotent to be a present blessing,
  I built fair castles for thy future bliss,
And more than ever prayed for gifts and
    goodness,
  That might contribute to thy happiness.

Oh, never may a wrong or reckless action
  Pollute the happy hand by thine caressed!
Nor ever thought or sentiment unworthy
  Tinge the proud cheek which thy dear lips
    have pressed!

As through the desolated rooms I wandered,
  To fill the void thy image kindly came;

The flickering shadows took thy form in fall-
    ing,
  The winds without were whispering thy
    name.

Thy cloak hung in the hall, I could not pass
    it ;
  More than all else it seemed a part of
    thee ;
Some potent spell it must have borrowed
    from thee,
  To draw me, draw me irresistibly.

I took it to my room and wrapped it round
    me,
  Closer and closer, as the storm grew loud ;
Sweetly and safely seemed it to enfold me,
  As though with thine own love and power
    endowed.

I laid my cheek against the velvet lining,
  Where late, I loved to fancy, thine had
    been ;

How could I fear, thus filled with thy dear
    influence,
  The storm without, the loneliness within!

To the wild winds it gave a softer cadence,
  A mellowing glory to the lightning gleams;
It filled the large and lonely room with ra-
    diance,
  And the long night with rich and rosy
    dreams.

IN MEMORY OF S. E. S.

TRUE manliness is never more apparent
    Than in defense of woman;
And thou, her invincible knight-errant,
    Revering in her the divine and human,

And scorning man's abuse of power and station,
    Emboldened her to choose her own career,
Hailing with generous appreciation
    All excellence of hers in every sphere.

In all the annals of chivalric daring
    What match for thy devotion can be found?
The knights of old, a carnal war declaring,
    For coarser deeds and weapons were re-
        nowned.

No risk was theirs of undervaluation,
    By all the amiable sex adored;

How could they match thy self-renunciation,
  Or wield thy weapon, mightier than the
    sword?

Thy faith and patience, almost superhuman,
  Beyond all barriers overlooked the goal,
The scorn of man, the indifference of woman,
  Meeting with imperturbable control.

Each year, with zeal and courage unabated,
  Thy struggle was renewed against the
    wrong;
No failure could discourage or embitter
  A heart and will so hopeful and so strong.

With such unwavering trust and patience
    gifted,
  Oh, what to thee were laurels and renown,
By foresight of the future good uplifted,
  Thy faith and zeal were both reward and
    crown.

January, 1889.

SENTIMENT.

WHY THUS LONGING?

Why thus longing, thus forever sighing,
  For the far-off, unattained and dim,
While the beautiful, all round thee lying,
  Offers up its low, perpetual hymn?

Wouldst thou listen to its gentle teaching,
  All thy restless yearnings it would still;
Leaf and flower and laden bee are preaching
  Thine own sphere, though humble, first to
    fill.

Poor indeed thou must be, if around thee
  Thou no ray of light and joy canst throw;
If no silken cord of love hath bound thee
  To some little world through weal and woe;

If no dear eyes thy fond love can brighten,
  No fond voices answer to thine own;

If no brother's sorrow thou canst lighten
  By daily sympathy and gentle tone.

Not by deeds that win the crowd's applauses,
  Not by works that give thee world-renown,
Not by martyrdom or vaunted crosses,
  Canst thou win and wear the immortal
    crown.

Daily struggling, though unloved and lonely,
  Every day a rich reward will give;
Thou wilt find, by hearty striving only,
  And truly loving, thou canst truly live.

Dost thou revel in the rosy morning,
  When all nature hails the lord of light,
And his smile, nor low nor lofty scorning,
  Gladdens hall and hovel, vale and height?

Other hands may grasp the field and forest,
  Proud proprietors in pomp may shine;
But with fervent love if thou adorest,
  Thou art wealthier, — all the world is thine!

Yet if through earth's wide domains thou
    rovest,
Sighing that they are not thine alone,
Not those fair fields, but thyself, thou lovest,
    And their beauty and thy wealth are gone.

Nature wears the colors of the spirit;
    Sweetly to her worshiper she sings;
All the glow, the grace, she doth inherit,
    Round her trusting child she fondly flings.

"FOR BEHOLD THE KINGDOM OF GOD IS WITHIN YOU."

Pilgrim to the heavenly city
  Groping wildered on thy way,
Look not to the outward landmarks,
  List not what the blind guides say.

For long years thou hast been seeking
  Some new idol found each day;
All that dazzled, all that glittered,
  Lured thee from the path away.

On the outward world relying,
  Earthly treasures thou wouldst heap;
Titled friends and lofty honors
  Lull thy higher hopes to sleep.

Thou art stored with worldly wisdom,
  All the lore of books is thine;

And within thy stately mansion
   Brightly sparkle wit and wine.

Richly droop the silken curtains
   Round those high and mirrored halls;
And on mossy Persian carpets
   Silently thy proud step falls.

Not the gentlest wind of heaven
   Dares too roughly fan thy brow,
Nor the morning's blessed sunbeams
   Tinge thy cheek with ruddy glow.

Yet 'midst all these outward riches,
   Has thy heart no void confessed —
Whispering, "Though each wish be granted,
   Still, oh still, I am not blessed"?

And when happy, careless children,
   Lured thee with their winning ways,
Thou hast sighed in vain contrition,
   "Give me back those golden days."

Hadst thou stooped to learn their lesson —
    Truthful preachers — they had told
Thou thy kingdom hast forsaken,
    Thou hast thine own birthright sold.

Thou art heir to vast possessions, —
    Up, and boldly claim thine own,
Seize the crown that waits thy wearing,
    Leap at once upon thy throne.

Look not to some cloudy mansion,
    'Mong the planets far away,
Trust not to the distant future,
    Let thy heaven begin to-day.

When thy struggling soul hath conquered,
    When the path lies fair and clear,
When thou art prepared for heaven,
    Thou wilt find that heaven is here.

SUPPLICATION.

Forgive me, Father, if I dared
  To doubt the justice of thy will;
The dark distrust, the murmurings mad,
  Father forgive, and guard me still.

Oh, save me from the inward strife,
  Where passion recklessly contends ·
With all the holier laws of life,
  And all the light religion lends.

Oh, save me from the lawless course,
  The impious thought, the rebel will,
And give me faith, and give me force,
  To trust in and obey thee still.

What storms of feeling yet may come,
  What losses I may yet survive,

Before I reach that peaceful home
  Where good and ill no longer strive,

Thou only knowest, and thou alone
  Canst guide and guard me safely through;
Help me to say, "Thy will be done,"
  And nerve me to endure and do.

Oh, let me feel, whate'er may come,
  I am not banished far from thee;
And all life's losses, all death's gloom,
  May teach some heavenly truth to me.

WORLDLY-MINDEDNESS.

O BOUNTEOUS world, against thy foes reviling,
  Thy earnest champion I have been for years,
Nor, little cause though I might have for smil-
    ing,
  Would I traduce thee as a vale of tears.

Even methinks within heaven's starry portals
  I might be homesick, thinking there of thee,
And angels I have known, though only mortals,
  As fair and good as I would wish to see.

And yet my love is not a blind adherence;
  Thy ills and errors I would help to mend,
Yet shrink with awe from hasty interference
  In plans too vast for me to comprehend.

Yet couldst thou know what dreams of high
    endeavor,

What golden visions of a destiny,
Fairer perhaps than any thou hast ever
   For thyself imaged, I have dreamed for
      thee;

Down the long ages picturing thy progression,
   Till all thy youthful errors are outgrown,
And Death is only as a dim tradition,
   A monster of the infant planet known;

How all thy revolutions and diseases
   Have seemed rude struggles after health
      and light,
How ready, when the actual displeases,
   My fancy is to take that " fond old flight ";

Thou mightst forgive if I have failed in doing,
   Nor deem it from a want of heart or
      will —
Though thankfully the smallest good pursuing,
   I long in larger ways to serve thee still.

MEMORIES.

When the daylight gently dying
  Lingers, as if loth to go,
And its busy din retreating
  Merges in a murmur low,
The strange power of that hour
  Magic spells around me throw.

From the present, from the actual,
  Swiftly I am borne away,
And in spirit through the wildwood
  Once again with thee I stray.
As I wander, ever fonder
  Holier influences sway.

Worldly wisdom, worldly maxims,
  All are banished at thy side,
Doubt and danger are forgotten,
  In the full resistless tide

Of sweet feeling, o'er me stealing,
    Which I do not care to hide.

How the magic of thy presence
    Robes the earth in hues divine;
One by one, the stars appearing,
    With strange lustre seem to shine;
Night's low noises hush their voices,
    At the melody of thine.

Fairer seems the world around us,
    Loftier the o'erarching sky;
And the air is filled with music,
    As the wild wind wanders by.
Life is dearer, heaven is nearer,
    O beloved! when thou art nigh.

LOVE.

O WANTON and gay little archer, to whom
 the world long time has given
 A name most sacred and dear, to our sweetest emotion applied,
How poorly to me dost thou image that angel descended from heaven,
 Familiar with sorrow and tears, and to all
  that is earnest allied.

O holy and beautiful spirit, what image could
 well represent thee?
 What sweet combination of words can portray that divinest idea?
Wherever thou art it is heaven, and merciful
 heaven has lent thee
 A solace for all that is sorrowful, unsatisfac-
  tory here.

ASPIRATION.

I HAD almost faltered by the wayside,
　　But sweet words have come to me of late,
Words at once so cheering, and so soothing,
　　They have nerved my heart for any fate.

Shall I linger in alluring places,
　　While my ideal ever urges on?
No, — my heart must never know reposing,
　　Till that far-off glittering goal is won.

Ah! 't were worth long years of patient striv-
　　　ing
　　Those receding realms to reach at last;
Can I not, from thence, new strength deriv-
　　　ing,
　　Burst the chains which bind my spirit fast?

Link by link, the serpent coil unwinding,
    Day by day some higher ground to win;
May I not, at last, O holy Father!
    Soar above all forms of death and sin?

And once more in thy clear presence living,
    Love thee, serve thee, live for thee alone?
Ah! this blessed hope will speed me onward,
    Till that glorious heaven is mine own.

PESSIMIST.

Never again will I be won to laud thee,
 O world! so siren-voiced, so seeming fair,
O mocking phantom! luring lovers towards
  thee,
 And fading, as they clasp thee, into air.

What beautiful new cheat wilt thou next
  offer,
 To win me from my fortress of disdain?
What cunning masquerade to make the scoffer
 Retract his scorn, and dream of love again?

Will not one sad thought of the past suffice
  us
  To scorn thy spells, and break thy golden
   chain?
And can thy sweet shows evermore entice us,
 While memories of their emptiness remain?

While might makes right, and all the op-
　pressed are weary
Waiting for mercy to unveil her face:
While freedom is a glorious thing in theory,
　But in the state quite out of date and
　place:

While modesty in books is much applauded,
　But trampled in the crowd and jostled by:
While work as holy mission oft is lauded,
　And all the weary workers left to die?

If, spite of all the discord that surrounds us,
　Love in our homes sweet household music
　makes;
When other hearts to life have strongly bound
　us,
　And earth is beautiful for their dear sakes;

When, though dark clouds above us thickly
　gather,
　Fond eyes make sunlight wheresoe'er we
　dwell;

Then death steps in, and silences forever
  The lips and eyes that we have loved so
    well.

And when at night we wildly ask of heaven,
  "Oh, shall we find them on the eternal
    shore?"
No answer to our earnest prayer is given;
  Only the night-winds sigh, "No more, no
    more."

Life in its gay and giddy vortex whirls us,
  Luring us with sweet promises and fair;
Then from the heights of hope and rapture
    hurls us,
  Down to the lowest depths of grim despair.

There we are left to struggle dimly upward,
  A weary way, in darkness and alone;
With no sweet hopes, like angels, beckoning
    forward,
  But haunting fears, fell demons, goading on.

Involved in mystery, all but death uncertain,
 We seek the future and the past to know;
But on all sides a dark, impervious curtain
 Shuts down to say, "No farther shalt thou
  go."

OPTIMIST.

O LIFE! O lovely luring life!
  In vain we seek to break thy fetters;
Thy roses may with thorns be rife,
  But we are still thy debtors.

Grant that the rose's reign is brief,
  Joy may be fleet, but pain is fleeter,
And fragrant dust of flower and leaf
  Make coming roses sweeter.

Life's garlands fade and fall too fast,
  But richer gains repair such losses;
Heaven saves its best gifts to the last,
  And life its finer forces.

In spite of all the dreary shrouds,
  In which care seeks to hide and bind us;
In spite of sorrow's lowering clouds,
  Hope's sunny glance will find us.

We may be warned against her wiles,
  And vow to entertain her never,
But irresistibly she smiles,
  And we are hers forever.

The song springs lightly to our lips
  That yesterday were mute with sorrow,
And happiness's brief eclipse
  But makes a brighter morrow.

The clouds that overhang the skies
  Will serve to make the heavens bluer;
And friends that fail and love that dies
  But show the faithful truer.

And even if souls esteemed the best
  In treachery be at last detected,
Truth's careful counterfeits attest
  How much she is respected.

We well may seem obscure and small
  In the vast universe of being,

But the welfare of each and all
  Is dear to the All-seeing.

One glance into the blue above,
  The depths of blue, so calm and holy,
Reveals to us a God of love,
  No God of justice solely.

And I must think, oft noting how
  Impartially his rays are given,
The pitifullest fiend below
  Must have some gleams of heaven.

The future, God alone can know,
  The present, he has kindly lent us;
And following him, where'er we go
  His angels will attend us.

Bounties so manifold and dear
  Should check the skeptic's scorn and laugh-
      ter;
If blind to all the blessings here,
  Can we deserve hereafter?

DREAM-LAND.

Day may boast of bounteous spirits,
　　All the airiest, brightest, best;
Ah! the night has one kind angel
　　That can rival all the rest.

Throw some magic spell around me,
　　O sweet sleep! that I may sing
All the wonders thou hast shown me,
　　All the wealth that thou canst bring.

Sorrow, like a dream, recedeth,
　　Tears and sins are washed away,
And night offers all we wildly,
　　Vainly prayed for through the day.

Then the coldest eyes beam kindly,
　　Sternest lips let fond words fall,

And the love so late despaired of
  Throws enchantment over all.

Then the dear familiar voices,
  Voices heard by day no more,
Fill the eyes with tearful gladness,
  Thrill the heart through, as of yore.

And with those so loved and longed for,
  Hand in hand, we gayly go
Over field where softened sunlight
  Gilds and hallows all below.

Then the clouds reveal fair faces,
  Strangely sweet the wind-harps play;
And the trees make human gestures,
  Mutely beckoning us away.

Till at last we reach exultant
  Those bright realms where joy has birth,
Those receding sunset regions
  Where the heavens kiss the earth.

Lovely land! the dazzling daylight
  Breaks too soon thy shadowy spell ;
Yet long after on the eyelids
  Thy sweet influences dwell.

Therefore 'wildering visions haunt us,
  'Mid the tumult of the day ;
But we pause to ask their meaning,
  And like ghosts they glide away.

UNDINE.

AND hast thou left this upper world forever,
  Dearest of visions, beautiful Undine?
Oh, with what earnest, with what fond en-
    deavor,
  My thoughts have followed thee to realms
    unseen!

Ever when bending o'er the deep blue sea,
  I look into its depth with eager longing,
For then the brightest, wildest dreams of
    thee,
  And of those crystal palaces come throng-
    ing.

And art thou gone forever? Oh, once more
  Come back, and take me with thee; let me
    go

Far from these skies and this familiar shore,
  Down, down, where sparkles thy bright
    home below;

With thee to wander 'neath the sunlight pale,
  Amid those beauties of the olden world,
Which the floods covered with their silver veil,
  While round their ruins loving sea-moss
    curled.

Deep in the shadow of those coral groves,
  Following thy footsteps o'er the sparkling
    sands,
I might imbibe thy universal love,
  And scorn the maxims cold of other lands.

Ah, trust me, I would leave behind me all
  Those narrow, forced, unnatural ways of
    thought,
Which like a sad weight on thy heart did
  fall.
  Chilling the soul thou hadst so dearly
    bought.

Thy deep affection no neglect could kill,
  That love so truthful, so almost divine ;
Oh, I would learn of thee, and worship, till
  My soul became as beautiful as thine !

Within my heart, dear Undine, there are
      chords
  That ever thrill responsive to thine own ;
I love the same wild sports, the haunted
      woods,
  The cliffs, where wild waves break in thun-
      der tones.

" The beings of the mind are not of clay,"
  And thou not all unreal because unseen ;
Thou livest wherever soul o'er sense bears
      sway,
  Imperishable, beautiful Undine !

AFTER READING "THE RAVEN."

Leave us not so dark, uncertain,
Lift again the fallen curtain,
Let us once again the mysteries
 Of that haunted room explore, —
Hear once more that friend infernal,
That grim visitor nocturnal,
Earnestly we long to learn all
  That befalls that bird of yore.
  Oh, then tell us something more!

Doth his shade thy floor still darken?
Dost thou still despairing hearken
To that deep sepulchral utterance,
 Like the oracles of yore?
In the same place is he sitting?
Does he give no sign of quitting,
Is he conscious, or unwitting,
  When he answers, " Nevermore "?
  Tell me truly, I implore!

Knows he not the littlenesses
That humanity possesses ?
Knows he never need of slumber,
   Fainting forces to restore ?
Stoops he not to eating, drinking ?
Is he never caught in winking,
When his demon eyes are sinking
   Deep into thy bosom's core ?
   Tell me this, if nothing more !

Is he after all so evil ?
Is it fair to call him devil ?
Did he not give friendly answer,
   When thy speech friend's meaning bore ?
When thy sad tones were revealing
All the loneness o'er thee stealing,
Did he not, with fellow-feeling,
   Vow to leave thee nevermore ?
   Keeps he not that oath he swore ?

He too may be inly praying,
Vainly, earnestly essaying

To forget some matchless mate,
   Beloved yet lost forevermore ;
He has donned a suit of mourning,
And all earthly comfort scorning,
Broods alone from night till morning.
   By thy memories of Lenore,
   Oh, renounce him nevermore !

Though he be a sable brother,
Treat him kindly as another ;
Ah ! perhaps the world has scorned him
   For that luckless hue he wore ;
No such narrow prejudices
Can he know whom love possesses,
Wrongs who willingly redresses,
   Do not spurn him from thy door,
   Lest love enter nevermore.

No bad bird of evil presage,
Happily be bears some message
From that much-mourned, matchless maiden.
   From that loved and lost Lenore.

In a pilgrim's garb disguisèd,
Angels are but seldom prizèd;
Of that fact at length advisèd,
　　Were it strange if he forswore
　　The false world forevermore?

O thou ill-starred midnight ranger,
Dark, forlorn, mysterious stranger,
Wildered wanderer from the Eternal,
　　Lighting on time's stormy shore:
Tell us of that world of wonder,
Of that famed, unfading yonder,
Rend, oh rend the veil asunder,
　　Let our fears and doubts be o'er!
　　Doth he answer, "Nevermore"?

WINTER NIGHTS.

In winter, when the nights were long,
   How short, how fleeting, seemed the hours!
Our carols filled the air with song,
   Our fancy decked the earth with flowers.

As to and fro, with twining arms
   And teeming brain, the rooms we paced,
Life lay before us rich in charms,
   No vale of tears, no desert waste;
And come whatever haps or harms,
   Our hearts and fates were interlaced.

In winter, when the nights were long,
   We dreamed of deeds transcending fame;
In fancy we would right all wrong,
   And even the great Dragon tame.

We told old stories weird and wild,
　　Till almost we believed them true;
And though at fear we mocked and smiled,
　　Closer and closer still we drew;
Watching, by fancy half beguiled,
　　The shadows which the firelight threw.

In winter, when the nights were long,
　　If they were cold we did not know,
For love and courage, beating strong,
　　Shed everywhere a summer glow.

On rosy apples, golden corn,
　　With snowy lining overcurled,
We feasted when the nights came on,
　　Content as if we owned the world;
And diamonds we dissolved might scorn
　　The fair Egyptian's famèd pearl.

In winter, when the nights were long,
　　The tempest's wrath we could defy;
And loved to hear its fitful song,
　　Now low and sad, now wild and high.

Round doors and windows vainly roaring,
   Secure we heard its varying play,
A rallying strain of triumph pouring,
   And then receding far away.
Our songs above the winds were soaring,
   Our hearts were merrier than they.

In winter, when the nights are long,
   Alone I wander to and fro;
Where are the hearts so light and strong?
   Where are the hopes of long ago?

Musing, I wander to and fro,
   While mournful memories round me throng;
Or else for solace chanting low
   Fragments of some familiar song
We learned together long ago,
   In winter, when the nights were long.

I listen for an echo soft,
   But no kind spirits condescend;
Only my own heart answers oft,
   " Patience, — the longest night will end."

HERE in this high and leafy hall,
Where the slanting sunbeams softly fall,
And the length'ning shadows come and go
O'er the undulating grass below,
Each odor, each tone, that round me strays
Recalls the green haunts of bygone days.
I tread once more in my childhood's track,
And its rosy hours come thronging back;
And gently and swiftly they bear me on,
Till the past and the present blend in one.

With bounding heart I am out once more
Where the fallen leaves play round the old
  farm door,
And dance to the music of the breeze
That sweeps through the old Balm o' Gilead
  trees.

I travel again the familiar ways,
In the wane of the warm September days;
I watch the sun go down at night,
And greet him at morn with a new delight,
Before he can kiss the dewy drops
From the violets' eyes, 'neath the shady copse.
Into the ground-sparrow's nest I peep,
While the morning-glory is fast asleep;
And when the declining sun is low,
And o'er the green earth sheds a golden glow,
Down to the river's bank I hie, —
Down o'er the interval, Nero and I.
No merry companions share our glee,
But nature speaks to us lovingly.
The grass bows low as we pass along,
The cricket sings us a happy song,
The flowers look up from their hiding-place,
The butterfly lures us to the chase,
The squirrel peeps out from behind the tree,
The branches are beckoning constantly,
And the leaves are whispering, "Come and
    see."

Before I know it the day is gone,
And night steals swiftly and silently on.
I see strange shapes in the woods around,
I start if an acorn fall to the ground;
The winds, with a lonesome, mournful tone,
Seem to whisper softly, "Summer is gone."
The branches borrow their notes of grief,
And chant a dirge o'er each fallen leaf,
While mysterious shadows flit silently by,
At each gush of the mournful melody.
I know 't is my own imagining,
Yet closer to Nero's side I cling;
Half fearful, half entranced, I stay,
Watching the moonbeams' fitful play,
Till the horn from the farm-house warns me
        back,
And Nero bounds on the homeward track.

Swiftly those holidays flew by,
And I turned to my books with a heavy sigh;
For their cold, stern pages offered not
The loftier lessons nature taught.

I cared not to learn their lore profound, —
Why the rosy apple fell to the ground,
Or the stars, long wakeful, one by one
Closed their sweet eyes from the dazzling sun.
Enough for me to feel and share
The beauty that met me everywhere;
Enough to feel, and to enjoy,
Without reflection's cold alloy.

POEM

THE sentiment the most divine and human,
    The oppressed and weak to cherish and de-
        fend,
The key-note is of the devoted woman
    Whom all her sex may proudly claim as
        friend.

Not hers the maxim by rude power respected,
    " From him that hath not shall be taken all."
Is any class by law left unprotected ?
    Their cause is hers, with them to stand or
        fall.

Not even their thankless scorn can irritate her,
    With power to embitter or impair
So radically sweet and strong a nature,
    Revealed in word and deed, in voice and air.

How potent are her powers of persuasion,
 All studied art and rhetoric above!
How just and eloquent her indignation,
 An anger beautiful and kin to love!

But adequate return or thanks to tender
 Is not for us, a humble, loving few;
In future years a grateful world will render
 Remorsefully the honor long her due.

Gladly we recognize her noble mission,
 But not by this a favor we confer,
For by a just and timely recognition
 Ourselves it is we honor more than her.

A. W. M.

STRANGEST contrasts blend in thee
With bewildering witchery :
Earnest aims, yet playful ways,
Turning work to holidays ;
Zeal impetuously impelling,
Cool discretion curbing, quelling ;
Words direct that hit the white
Like a searching line of light ;
Candor that can ne'er conceal,
Words that wound and deeds that heal ;
Bantering airs that ill accord
With a dress severe and odd ;
Feelings warm, and judgment cool,
The heart to serve, the mind to rule.

H. M. P.

Loveliest of all gifts has she,
Large and tender sympathy.
In your very moodiest mood
She can tenderly intrude,
And all medicine beyond
Lift you from the " Slough Despond ; "
For her nature, large and fine,
Can all men and moods divine;
All your wrongs before they 're shown
She will fondly make her own;
All your failings she avers
Lovingly are likewise hers,
And in that attractive light
You begin to love them quite.
Though with all that 's best imbued
She is never " unco gude."

TO HARRIET.

When long ago, O sweetest friend, I found
    thee,
  How little could my childish heart divine
The love-inspiring influence around thee,
    The blessings then in store for me through
    thine!

The counsel wise, the ready aid unfailing,
  The sympathy spontaneous and free,
And over all the affluent love prevailing,
  And like a magnet drawing all to thee.

Thy keen discernment and appreciation,
  All good in others quickly to divine,
Are mated by the ready indignation
  With which their wrongs are tenderly made
    thine.

When sorrow came the fondest ties to sever,
　When my benighted eyes no cheer could see,
Straining for gleams of heaven with vain en-
　　deavor,
　What has thy clearer vision been to me!

When to my dimmed eyes came no revela-
　　tions,
　Consoling visions have I had through thine;
The example of thy touching trust and patience,
　How often has it stimulated mine!

How without uttered word, like warmth per-
　　vading,
　Thy very presence has serenely wrought,
Dispelling doubt and to all peace persuading,
　A soothing balm to my rebellious thought!

And thus is the ascending path made clearer,
　And discord is resolved in harmony;
The far-off heaven, O beloved, is nearer,
　And earth more precious for the thought of
　　thee.

LUCRETIA MOTT AND LYDIA MARIA CHILD.

In the great moral conflict of our nation,
  Two forms are eminent the strife above,
Divinely blending manly force and courage
  With all a woman's tenderness and love.

They walked unflinching where e'en heroes
      faltered,
    They braved with smiling front the world's
      dread scorn,
They found their rest in earnest toil for others,
  They found their joy in helping the forlorn.

Their urgent and resistless force of feeling
  Was held in sway by equal force of mind,
And always were their words and acts revealing
  Wisdom and love harmoniously combined.

This harmony will echo and reëcho,
　Though their belovèd forms no more we see,
Their words and deeds are still our benedic-
　　tion,
　Their lives inspire us perpetually.

Still shines their light to elevate and cheer us,
　We feel their influence serene and strong;
Better and happier are our lives forever
　That we have known them and have loved
　　them long.

CONSOLA.

THE worldling oft in curious wonder glances
  At the meek air of quiet Quakeress,
But ne'er divines the rebel thoughts and fan-
    cies
  That riot 'neath that placid mien and dress.

Consola, reared with tender supervision,
  In strict conformance to the Quaker rules,
Confessed to many a treacherous intuition
  Never yet learned or unlearned in the schools.

Forbidden longings, innocent and human,
  She, secretly impenitent, repressed;
For, hovering still between the child and
    woman,
  She had not found the courage to protest.

An eye had she for all the alluring graces,
  For air, and dress by pretty worldlings
    worn —
The flowing fall of ribbons, robes, and laces,
  The tints that mock the sunset and the
    dawn.

She was content to enjoy this decoration —
  Or tried to be — in others' dress alone,
But ventured on one little innovation
  To mitigate the primness of her own.

Deftly a silken pocket she embroidered,
  To don, or doff if elders thought it sin ;
And lovingly she o'er the labor loitered,
  Weaving her fancies and her hopes therein.

Would Luther notice it, and think it pretty?
  Would he like rose, or blue, or lilac best?
Or would he criticise, and think — oh, pity ! —
  Her heart by foolish vanity possessed?

Luther at meeting waited her arrival,
　Knew the old bay, and helped her to alight;
But what he saw was not the embroidered trifle,
　Had it been twenty times as fair and
　　bright.

He saw the blue eyes by long lashes shaded,
　Whose speaking power enhanced the charm
　　of words
That seemed to sweetest music modulated,
　Dearer to him than morning song of birds.

He saw the roseate glow that, coming, going,
　Unconsciously revealed each varying mood;
The ruling one an artless overflowing
　Of loving-kindness and solicitude.

Long had he sought in vain for an occasion
　To tell his love, and this day he had
　　planned
To leave a simple written declaration
　Safely within her little greeting hand.

But watchful eyes in close approximation
  Thwarted his dear design, and, sorely tried,
On entering church, with sudden desperation,
  He dropped it in the pocket at her side.

She, all unconscious of its intervention,
  To serious things devoutly turned her
      thought,
And soon commanded her enrapt attention
  The ministration of Lucretia Mott.

With eloquent, persuasive exhortation
  She pictured slavery, its woe and sin,
And roused the conscience of the congrega-
    tion
  To feel its own complicity therein.

Consola, with the gentle sect to screen her,
  Had little known of suffering, wrong, or
     thrall,
And all the woman dormant yet within her
  Rose in response to that resistless call.

It lent new force to long-accepted teaching,
  To life and love a larger meaning gave;
And leaving church, she said, with eyes be-
    seeching,
  "O Luther, let us labor for the slave!"

At home, her former mood severely scorning,
  The embroidered bauble far away she
    tossed,
And, gathered up with refuse of the morn-
    ing
  By accident 't was carried off and lost.

Luther, endeavoring to frame excuses
  That might explain a silence so remiss,
Forgiving, said, " The tender heart refuses
  To answer no, yet cannot answer yes."

But with his grief he manfully contended,
  And all his youthful force and fervor threw
Into the larger struggle which impended, —
  The cause of Freedom, and Consola's too.

Together, with indomitable ardor,
　They breasted prejudice, they laughed at
　　scorn,
While he, solicitous to guide and guard her,
　Smoothed the rough path, intent to help or
　　warn.

To this enlarging labor dedicated,
　They daily grew in a diviner grace,
And into words far-reaching he translated
　The appealing pity of her speaking face.

The sudden vision of a sweeter blessing
　Would sometimes gleam athwart them and
　　above,
While in each other's friendship still confessing
　A dearer charm than any other's love ;

Until, in an old chest by chance neglected,
　After four years of earnest effort passed,
Its precious contents safe and unsuspected,
　The long-lost pocket came to light at last.

And then the past rose clear and plain before
      her, —
  His oft-revealed but ne'er-intruded love,
His fending foresight like an ægis o'er her,
  His ready sympathy even help above.

She sought him soon, confusedly explaining
  How on that day the pocket went astray,
And now was found; but here, her courage
      waning,
    She paused, and turned her tell-tale face
    away.

He flushed, then paled, with doubt and long-
     ing rifted,
  And while hope wavering still seemed afar,
Her tearful tender eyes to his she lifted,
  Revealing heaven — with the gates ajar.

NATURE.

SHE comes! the universe awakes to greet her,
  With rapturous joy the heart of nature
    thrills ;
Bright thoughts and buoyant hopes leap forth
    to meet her,
  And life, at her warm glance, the faint heart
    fills.

The heavens reflect the azure of her eye,
  The earth gives back her sweet and radiant
    smile,
The winds and waters to her voice reply,
  And chant the measure of her step mean-
    while.

Her airy foot-falls scarcely brush the dews,
  And leave, where'er they light, a greener
    trace ;

Her radiant eyes give to the flowers their
  hues,
    Her breath their fragrance, and her touch
      their grace.

Her lustrous hair has caught the sun's bright
  beams,
    And robbed them of their gay and golden
      store;
The rainbow she hath rifled, and it seems,
    Enrobing her, to win one grace the more.

Darkness and sin, beneath her searching
  glances,
    Shrink swiftly, cowering and abashed, away,
And fear and cankered care, as she advances,
    Vanish like phantoms that avoid the day.

She passes on, and ever in her train
    Follows a joyous troop of rosy hours;
O'er pride and luxury, misery and pain,
    O'er rich and poor alike, her wealth she
      showers.

She stops not at the mansions of the great,
   She gladdens the poor sinner's lonely cell;
She lights the lowly hut, the halls of state,
   And lingers fondly where her lovers dwell.

Gently she passes from the world away,
   And the earth seems a shade less fair and
     young;
Yet memory of her, throughout the day,
   Speeds lightly all the after hours along.

But daylight dies, and lo! a loftier presence
   Fills the green courts where late her reign
     hath been;
Her subjects all forsake their old allegiance,
   And offer homage to a rival queen.

She comes not like her younger sister, calling
   The world to welcome her with song and
     dance,
Lightly and noiselessly her spells are falling,
   And the awed earth is hushed beneath her
     glance.

A holier radiance lights her earnest eye,
    A heavenly halo crowns her paler brow;
The sense was then a captive willingly,
    The soul bows down with deeper reverence
        now.

The moon and stars attend her on her way,
    And by their pale and mystic light reveal
The grace her every motion doth betray,
    The form her shadowy robes would fain
        conceal.

At her approach, the flowers, bending low,
    Incline their graceful heads in silent prayer,
And while her gentle hands sweet dews be-
        stow,
    Their fragrant lips anoint her trailing hair.

She brings dear visions to the homesick mind,
    And welcome rest to the o'erwearied limbs;
She gives a foretaste of those realms divine
    Whose glory and whose purity she hymns.

Like some sweet strain of music sad and low,
　Her presence moves the inmost soul, and
　　seems
To waken memories of long ago,
　To image the beloved we meet in dreams.

All high and holy mysteries attend her,
　All gentle influences round her throng,
And spiritual beings freely lend her
　The glory that to their own spheres belong.

Kind angel! without thy alternate reign,
　Morn were no longer beautiful and bright ;
Her sunniest smile and glance, her sweetest
　　strain,
　Her dearest spell she owes to thee, O Night !

MORNING.

O'er hill and valley the young day is breaking,
  The waters dancing in the morning beams;
With eager step my couch and home forsaking,
  I share the joy which through all nature
    streams.

The flowers from their grassy beds are peeping,
  Roused by the kisses of the sun's warm
    rays;
The choir of birds, melodious chorus keeping,
  Make the woods vocal with their notes of
    praise.

O morning sun! my heart too leaps to greet
    thee,
  And like the flowers I revel in thy ray.
Ah! those who, dallying, do not rise to meet
    thee
  Lose the best hours of the golden day.

THE ROSE.

Once more art thou come to delight us, O
    lovely and long-looked-for wonder!
  All has been ready and waiting, impatient
    thy advent to see.
The sunbeams, for thee, long ago broke the
    fetters of winter asunder,
  The breezes have softened to sighing, the
    hard earth grown tender for thee.

The flowers that blossomed before thee were
    but thy attendants in waiting,
  Were only thy prophets and heralds, fore-
    telling, announcing, their queen ;
The season, progressive in beauty, at last in
    the Rose culminating,
  Is stayed by thy perfect completeness, con-
    tent on her laurels to lean.

I know why in June the sun's glances grow
 ever more ardent and stronger,
  I know why so radiant the mornings, so long
   and so lustrous the days,
Because the sun lingers at even to look on
 thy loveliness longer,
  And hurries the dawn to renew his all-thrill·
   ing, insatiate gaze.

O thou in all ages and nations sweet symbol of
 sweetest emotion !
  The synonym almost of joy is the tint which
   the world to thee owes ;
And when we would wish for our darling the
 fairest and happiest portion,
  We say, " Be her path strewn with roses, her
   future be couleur de rose."

THE ROSE.

Ah, gentle maiden, why
Pass me so lightly by,
Deeming me destitute of sense and soul?
More lavishly endowed
Than my contemners proud,
I hear in song the stars and seasons roll.

Low voices greet mine ear
That mortals may not hear,
Music their duller sense has never known;
I hold most sweet discourse
With life's mysterious source,
And yield obedience unto God alone.

Nature reveals to me
Much hidden mystery,
She speaks a language which no school has
taught:

Her voices sweet and clear
Proud man can never hear,
Audible only to the pure in thought.

I bathe in floods of light,
And from the hand of night
I drink inspiring draughts of crystal dew;
Nor care, nor toil, nor strife,
Invade my charmèd life,
I wake each morn to rapture ever new.

I know no selfish love,
All pride, all shame above,
My being freely do I offer up;
I taste ethereal bliss
In the sweet zephyr's kiss,
And give back incense from my dewy cup.

Laden with that rich freight,
On mortals he may wait,
And give my fragrant store of sweets away;

Again when he returns,
My heart with rapture burns,
Again I offer all, nor ask repay.

I do not waste my life,
With such pure pleasure rife,
In idle longings for some higher part;
The present is to me
An immortality,
And heaven bends low and reigns within my
heart.

I know, though I am gone,
The rose will still live on,
The soul, the beauty, I now body forth;
Immortal and divine,
In other forms than mine,
Will still add glory to the glorious earth.

THE COLUMBINE.

By the rugged rocks where the mosses grow,
Its wild and airy nooks I know.
The craggy rocks that were else forlorn
It loves to cling to and adorn.
Dearer that firm friend, stern and strong,
Than the yielding turf where the lowlands
     throng;
Dearer by far that rude retreat,
With the mosses clustering round its feet,
Than the bordered bed, where tender hands
Foster the flowers of far-off lands.

Reared by the rude rock, nursed by the rain,
Rocked to rest by the wind's wild strain,
Fair and flexile, yet fearless and free,
A fetterless child of the mountain, she.

No garden wall may her beauties bind,
She is wooed in turn by every wind.
But to all the rude North Wind may say
She will shake her willful head alway.
If in ire he threaten and rave and roar,
She will only shake her head the more.
Sometimes, to evade the wrathful storm,
She will bend to earth her willowy form,
Feigning a moment relenting mood,
Seemingly sorry and subdued,
Then spring erect with an airy grace,
And shake her head in his very face.

The sweet South Wind, with his gentle sway
And soft, insinuating way,
And alluring tales of his native clime,
Where the flowerets dread no winter time,
She will graciously hear; but, when all is said,
She only hangs her graceful head.
I know not whether this favorite wile
Is to hide a blush or to hide a smile;
But, for all the sweet South Wind may say,
He wears no favor of hers away.

I cannot say; but it seems to me
She reserves her sweets for the wandering bee,
Or a tuneful lover, brilliant and bold,
Who wears her own colors of scarlet and
    gold,
And flitted around her one morning in May,
And kissed the dew from her lips away,
And won her ear and her heart so free
By the magic might of his minstrelsy.
I know by his pausing, and listening long,
That the flower returned him song for song;
But my coarser sense essayed in vain
To catch that fine, aerial strain.

Sometimes, when Morning flings on high
Her rosy banners o'er all the sky,
I have thought I could hear the joyous shout
Which all those beautiful bells ring out;
But, soon as they hear my approaching foot,
The chime has ceased, the flower is mute.

I am loath to believe it; but it may be
They regard me as their enemy,

Because I invade their wild retreat,
And carry away the fair and sweet,
The freshest and fairest cull with care,
To make my chamber fresh and fair.
I wish I could make the darlings know
It is only because I love them so.

Though I treat them ever so tenderly,
I may seem to them as Death seems to me, —
A ruthless monster with evil eye,
Who passes the worn and the weary by,
And snatches away from Love's cherishing
      fold,
To illumine his cavern so lonesome and cold,
The dearest bloom in Love's sun unfurled,
Whose eye was the light of a little world,
And whose warmth and glow flung over all
A magic and resistless thrall.

O dread destroyer, tell me not
That only through thee may heaven be sought;

For when summer comes with bloom and song,
When dawns are rosy and days are long,
Then, but for thy retinue and thee,
Earth would be heaven enough for me.

THE WOODS OF MELROSE.

AGAIN, O you dear forest trees,
  For your companionship I yearn;
The longing love which you appease
  I fondly fancy you return.

For when I left you yestermorn,
  And cast a lingering look behind,
Your gestures beckoned my return,
  Your calls came to me on the wind.

Oh still I hear those sweet recalls,
  The extended arms I seem to see,
And long to leave the city walls,
  And fly, dear Melrose, back to thee.

THE FLOWER HUNT.

THE flowers awoke one summer's day,
By a shadowy river far away,
And each shook off the dew-drops bright,
And whispered softly its dream of the night.

The harebell that grew on the mountain's side
Was the first to ring an alarum wide,
Then looking down on the flowers below,
And shaking its bright head to and fro,

The vision it told with mysterious air,
For much of wonder and fear were there ;
And its sisters looked up with admiring eyes,
For its sweet face mirrored the clear blue
        skies.

The fairy that slept in its azure bell,
And left it just at the midnight knell,

A warning had breathed with its last adieu,
That chilled the hearts of the flowery crew:

" Renew not to-morrow your love and bliss,
Dream not to-night of the butterfly's kiss;
For before another sun shall set
A fearful foe must be shunned or met."

Then every flower, with tear-drops hung,
Its morning melody sadly sung;
For each had a boding dream to tell,
Which chimed with the peal of the blue hare-
    bell.

Oh! the woodland moaned then mournfully,
Like the troubled waves of the wind - swept
    sea;
And leaf and flower rocked to and fro
In a tremulous dread of coming woe.

A council of war was held straightway,
But whence the foe no seer could say;

And a strife arose which was sad to see,
Among flowers that had lived so lovingly.

The thistle lifted its purple crown,
And threatened to put all its rivals down;
With spears all pointed, and armor tight,
It claimed the lead as its natural right.
But the listeners laughed with republican scorn,
When it boasted of being nobly born.

In idle debate the time flew by,
Till the sun in the clouded heavens rode high,
And the flowers trembled at every sound,
As the woe-fraught hours were rolling round.

At length on the hushed and listening air
A murmur was borne to the tremblers there;
At first like the distant waving of trees,
Then nearer and louder it came on the breeze.

Light laughter peals rang merrily out,
And the echoing hills gave back the shout;

To the flowerets all, ah! sound of fear,
For they knew too well the hunters were near.

From afar they had scented the delicate game,
And onward in cruel haste they came
With song and jest, in girlish sport,
Unmindful of the dread they wrought.

Little hunting gear the troop displayed,
Their only arms a tiny blade,
And a delicate cord to bind their prey,
Which the wooing winds might lure away.

Each flower shrank to the darkest place,
Lamenting too late its lovely face,
And vainly tried to subdue or hide
The brilliant hues that were once its pride.

The wild rose caught the first maiden's glance,
And paled at sight of her unsheathed lance.
With remorseless haste the blade she drew,
Her eager aim was fatally true;

The rose's prayer was unheeded, unheard,
And fluttering it fell like a wounded bird.

Poor fated thing, 't was the latest comer,
The last and the loveliest rose of summer;
Its blushing leaves were but just unfurled,
It was loath to leave the lovely world.

The clematis twined round the nearest tree,
And thought to escape captivity;
Wildly and lovingly it clung,
When the spoiler's grasp all its tendrils wrung.

Close and closer, ah, vain endeavor!
They were parted to meet no more forever;
Its beautiful blossoms were wreathed in the
        curls
And round the hats of the reckless girls.

The humming-bird had been whispering low
To the honeysuckle, the long day through;
The bee had courted the clover blossom,
And nestled close to its bounteous bosom;

And the laurel opened its honey cell
To the butterfly it loved so well,
But when danger came the lovers had flown,
And the flowers were left to die alone.

The water-lily had lifted up,
On the lake's calm bosom, its snowy cup,
And with fearless air it floated there,
For to brave the deep no maiden dare.

They marked its grace with wistful eye,
As its fragrant breath on the air came by;
And the lily laughed low their despair to
    see,
And unfolded its petals coquettishly.

Dearly the thistle sold its life,
For the blood of the slayer flowed in the strife;
It cast one dying look around,
And saw all its humbler comrades bound.

The proud and the meek were alike laid low,
In the stern democracy of woe;

The blue-eyed grass, and the mountain's pride,
And the lady's slipper lay side by side.

The stately laurel bled on the sod,
With the buttercup and the golden-rod;
And the plebeian dandelion fell,
By the same rude hand, with the blue harebell.

Their incense no more at the sun's first rays
Will they offer up to their Author's praise;
No more will they start from their morning
      dream,
Their toilet to make in the silver stream.

The morn rose sad o'er the desolate scene,
To gaze on the spot where the spoilers had been;
And the river with mournful song flowed on,
Lamenting the beauty and love that had gone.

The flowers, meanwhile, all bound and wayworn,
In the captors' train were triumphantly borne;
But few survived to reach the place
Their beauty and odor were meant to grace.

Some perished with grief, from their loved ones
     torn ;
Others fainted with fear ere the march was
     done ;
The fairest, the sweetest, the greenwood's pride,
All hung their beautiful heads, and died.

SEPTEMBER.

Lend me fit strains to echo thy renown
    Ere thy sweet voices on the ear have died,
O golden season! even in thy frown
    More beautiful than all the year beside.

At thy approach, the sun, that wantonly
    Had parched the fair earth with his fiery eye,
Stands reverently off, and ventures only
    To kiss thy kirtle as thou passest by.

Thee e'en the frost spirit has no heart to harm;
    He lays his icy fingers lightly on,
And, adding to thy dower another charm,
    Delays his work of death till thou art gone.

The blue sky lovingly around thee closes,
    The heavens look fondly down, and seem
        more near,

Thou lackest only June's sweet wreath of
    roses,
  Dear month, to crown thee queen of all the
    year.

AUTUMN.

O SADDEST, sweetest season of the year,
    O wildest, loveliest time, all times excelling,
Though every smile of thine conceals a tear,
    And every wind a sorrow seems foretelling!

O wildest, loveliest time of all the year,
    When the leaves turn, and the turned leaves
        are falling,
What pains, what pleasures, sacred, blest, and
        dear,
    Thy scenes and thy wild voices are recalling!

Thy purple pomp at dawn is written o'er
    With sweet associations, sad and solemn;
Thy evening skies recall for evermore
    The dear eyes that have gazed so fondly on
        them.

Thy wild winds whisper strange, mysterious
    things,
Weird wonders, never told in olden story;
Thy golden sunsets shame the pomp of kings,
    And flood earth's fading fields with heaven's
    glory.

All soft and radiant hues unite to deck thee,
    All thrilling tones make musical thy reign;
And though with crowding tears I often greet
    thee,
    Such tears I willingly would weep again.

The melodies of Spring-time may be gayer,
    And laughing Summer rosier garlands wear;
O Autumn, mightier spells around thee gather,
    And Life and Death unite to make thee fair!

1845.

WINTER'S TRIUMPH.

EARTH had lost her verdant mantle,
Drear and bare stood bush and tree,
    Ghostlike wailing,
    Unavailing,
Their departed pageantry.

From the desolated forest,
From the sad earth, brown and dry,
    Night winds borrow
    Song of sorrow,
Waft it upwards to the sky.

" Not alone for vanished glory
And departed power we moan ;
    When we render
    All our splendor,
Then our lovers too have flown.

" All our green haunts are forsaken,
  And in lighted halls they boast
           Flowers fairer,
           Jewels rarer,
  Than the glory we have lost.

" All the gems of earth and ocean
  Art has cunningly combined,
           And bereft us,
           Till is left us
  Not a votary behind."

Pityingly the heavens listened,
Tenderly the skies bent down,
           Lowly bending,
           Earthward sending
Tears of sympathy profound.

Then the clouds all leagued together,
Each some friendly force employs,
           And that frost-sprite
           Who by starlight
Works such wonders without noise.

"Earth, dear mother! we will deck her,
We will make her cause our own;
    Regal splendor
    We will lend her,
Such as art has never known."

Cheerly on the task they entered,
Noiselessly their soft strokes fell,
    But by morning,
    Without warning,
Lo! a wondrous miracle.

Field and forest, rock and river,
Purest diamonds displayed;
    Frail and airy,
    Work of fairy
Never more amazement made.

Emerald, amethyst, and ruby
Blent their hues with diamond sheen;
    When the sun rose,
    Radiant rainbows
Were in each clear crystal seen.

Marble pavement, smoother, purer
Than in Persian tales you meet;
  Hall ne'er offered,
  Palace proffered,
Fairer floor for monarch's feet.

Gothic arch, with diamond columns,
Glittered through the spacious hall;
  Sparkling fountains,
  From the mountains,
Turned to crystals in their fall.

Art shrunk back with awe and wonder,
And the most insensate felt,
  At that hour,
  Beauty's power,
And at Nature's altar knelt.

Many days their weight of splendor
Shrub and tree in triumph wore;
  Thousands gazing,
  Thousands praising, —
Could they wish or ask for more?

"Oh, take back this heartless glitter!
Riches are a weight of woe ;
    They will cost us, —
    They have lost us
Ease and freedom, — let them go!"

Then the warm and genial sunbeams
Melted all that cold display,
    Like all glory,
    Transitory,
Fading into mist away.

1845.

FANCY.

LITTLE MARGERY.

What is the secret of her sway,
  This little queen without resources?
She has not strength, she has not wealth,
  And no array of armèd forces.

She has no wisdom, yet the wise
  Bow down submissively before her;
No jeweled crown to daze all eyes,
  Yet is she welcomed like Aurora.

No armèd forces did I say?
  With two soft arms this small magician
Has but to beckon, and straightway
  A host is at her disposition.

No jewels? Where can gems be found
  Of her dark eyes to match the wonder,

In whose unfathomable depth
  Are all the riches of Golconda?

No wealth has she?   In love alone
  So cunningly has she invested
That ten times ten per cent, returns
  Her wealth and wisdom have attested.

1886.

TO E. F.

Oh fly, little card, over hill and vale,
  On the wings of the wind away,
To the beautiful city in morning land
  In the arms of Casco Bay.

And carry my love to a dear little maid,
  A sweet little friend of mine ;
For 't is she I choose, if she 'll not refuse,
  To be my Valentine.

REPLY TO A VALENTINE.

FROM E. W. F.

DEAREST little friend of mine,
Wouldst thou be my Valentine?
For the kiss that came to me,
I will send back one, two, three —
Three of mine are merely meet
Pay for one so dainty sweet.

Something I should like to send
To my darling little friend
That would make his sweet blue eyes
Open wide with glad surprise.
Naught I know in earth or air
That would be too fine or fair.
I would drain the affluent sea,
Little darling, all for thee;

Flowers none so fair or sweet
I would scatter at thy feet,
And would fill thy little hands
With the fruit of sunny lands.
But instead of fruit and flowers
Round me fall the wintry showers;
So that, after wishing long,
I can only send a song.

TEN LITTLE HUMMING-BIRDS.

Ten little humming-birds flying forth to dine,
One of them ate too much, then there were but
    nine.
Nine little robins searching for a mate,
One of them was married, then there were but
    eight.
Eight little skylarks soaring up to heaven,
One of them stayed there, then there were but
    seven.
Seven little cherry-birds getting in a fix,
One could not get out again, then there were
    but six.
Six little ducklings going in to dive,
One sailed down the river, then there were but
    five.
Five little sparrows peeping in at the church
    door,
One went in to hear the music, then there but
    four.

Four little nestlings could not all agree,
One of them fell out, and then there were but
    three.
Three little swallows in a chimney flue,
One went down to see the folks, then there
    were but two.
Two little owlets hooting to the moon,
One became a lunatic, then there was but one.
One little whippoorwill sitting on a stone,
Singing through the long night, "I am all
    alone."

MY WINGS.

LET angels wear, at Art's decree,
　The eagle's ponderous pinions,
And nondescriptal hybrids be
　'Twixt fowl and fair dominions;

For me a less imposing pair,
　A humbler flight suffices;
My wings upon my feet I wear,
　As Mercury's device is.

And when the winds add theirs to mine,
　And come from favoring quarters,
As he o'erflies with his the skies,
　So I with mine the waters.

Their magic strokes, like fairy's wand,
　To warmer realms transport me,

And fairer openings beyond
  Flash luringly athwart me;

And bluer heavens above me bend,
  And softer winds attend me,
And spell-bound deeps their service lend
  To forward and befriend me.

The waters from their wintry walls
  Seem into billows breaking,
The snow-drifts change to foamy falls,
  The woods to life are waking,

And haste to meet me in my flight,
  And, all my joy repeating,
Wave with delight their summits bright,
  And bend to give me greeting.

When poised upon my wings I float,
  The blue above and under,
The earth each moment more remote,
  More near the world of wonder;

And all the winds come sweeping by,
  With spirit voices freighted,
I wonder, with delight, if I
  Am dreaming or translated.

CHARADE.

(HAREBELL.)

My first in freedom loves to play
  Where forest leaves are falling,
Startled at every sound astray,
  Or woodland voices calling;
Among the fern leaves far away,
  With the wild winds a ranger,
Almost as airy fleet as they
  At any thought of danger.

My second on all festal days
  Rings out a joyous clamor;
The toiler leaves his weary ways,
  The school-boy drops his grammar.
It speaks in solemn, warning tones,
  Whene'er the people need them,
But pours in annual jubilee
  Its loudest peal for freedom.

My whole, along the green hillside
  And through the mountain passes,
Inclines its graceful head to greet
  The little country lasses.
The graceful grasses at its feet
  For downward glances bless it;
It only lifts its blue eyes sweet,
  When the wild winds caress it.

CHRISTMAS CARDS.

(WITH FLOWERS.)

WINTRY skies may threat and lower,
   And the snow in hills be hurled;
Love can conjure leaf and flower,
   Love will warm the world.

(WITH SCISSORS.)

May this little token be an emblem
   Of the tender love between us twain,
Feeling a bond of union even when parted,
   And parted but to quickly meet again.

Though stern winter with icy chains
   Fetters land and sea,
In my heart perpetual summer reigns
   At the thought of thee.

What can I send
To my darling friend
All beautiful gifts above ;
With all that is sweetest and best
Already divinely blest,
What can I send but love !

Relentlessly each rolling year
Of some old friend bereaves us,
But the contracting circle brings more near
And makes more indispensable and dear
The few that heaven leaves us.

WITH BIRDS.

'T is love inspires us and elates,
    In every season song impelling ;
Love every little throat inflates,
    And all our songs of love are telling.

www.ingramcontent.com/pod-product-compliance
Lightning Source LLC
Chambersburg PA
CBHW020543270326
41927CB00006B/698